Just Us Girls

A Lighthearted Look
at the Friendships We Share

Written by Julie Sutton
Illustrated by Angela Jarecki

_____

To

_____

From

Just Us Girls

It's a fact of life, women need other women. Whether she's sharing your chocolate mousse or listening outside the fitting room curtain while you agonize over orange peel thighs, a good girlfriend is indispensable. Crisis, chaos, and stress seem much more bearable when shared with a friend. And let's face it. There are some things only understood by...

Just Us Girls

If it's really important, always seek a
woman's point of view. After all, can you
really trust advice from someone who
uses the same soap for both
his face and hands?

Your friendship is better than chocolate!

Well...anyway, it's right up there!

Friends are those special people

you can enjoy just doing nothing with...

and I'm always looking for a

good excuse to do nothing!

Of course you can eat it—
you just have to count it as
two breads, one dairy, and
150 optional calories.

GIRLFRIENDS...

figure there's cause for alarm

if you go a day without calling.

The way I see it,

the quality of a friendship

is in direct proportion to

the danger of losing bladder control

when she gets you laughing.

God created the earth in seven days,

and He parted the Red Sea...

I shouldn't be surprised He gave

me a wonderful friend like you!

You know me so well

you can finish my–

antique furniture for me!

Hah! Tricked ya!

Friends don't let friends
wear horizontal stripes
across the hips.

With age comes wisdom...

Gray hair is like a silver crown...

Wrinkles are a badge of honor...

Keep repeating these until you believe them.

So then, banish anxiety from your heart
and cast off the troubles of your body.

ECCLESIASTES 11:10 NIV

There are friends you call on

when you're in trouble,

and there are friends you call

to share a good laugh.

Thankfully, you're the

handy, all-purpose kind!

GIRLFRIENDS...

don't go shopping when one of them

needs something—are you kidding?

Where's the
fun in that?

I don't know about you, but I think

we'd have fewer "bad hair days"

if we weren't trying to

wear so many hats!

Knock-knock.

Who's there?

A 3000-calorie diet you can

actually lose weight on....

Yeah, that's a joke.

You inspire me to climb

to greater heights,

to seek out adventure,

to discover new horizons,

to face daunting challenges....

One of these days, I may even

take on thong underwear!

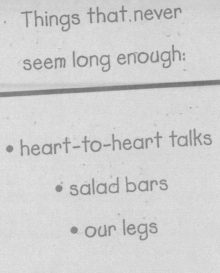

Things that never seem long enough:

- heart-to-heart talks
- salad bars
- our legs

Things that always
seem too long:

- grocery store
check-out lines
- boring committee
meetings
- the days between
"girls' night out"

It's like having my own personal
Good Samaritan on speed dial.

GIRLFRIENDS...

know that the best conversations happen

when you called for no particular reason.

You're such a heavenly friend!

Did you take lessons from the angels...

or are you winging it?

Hey! Did you know that today is

National Chocolate Appreciation Day?

Actually, there's no such holiday, but

I celebrate it every day anyway.

On the sixth day God created man.

Later He decided to create woman...

He was tired of Adam getting lost

in the Garden and refusing to ask

for directions.

GIRLFRIENDS...

understand why you will gladly abandon

cleaning your messy closets in order to

rummage through someone else's

second-hand "junk."

Warning: PMS...Personality

Mutating Strangely

You and I have learned

the secret of survival...

Pray softly and carry a big purse.

I can't seem to lose weight no matter

how many "light" foods I eat.

I'm beginning to think "LOWER IN FAT"

just refers to which half

of your body it lands on.

We women have a sixth sense about each other's needs. We understand the value of a comforting word, a heartfelt prayer, a reassuring smile... a quart of Ben & Jerry's.

GIRLFRIENDS...

take road trips without keeping track of either gas mileage or bathroom breaks!

How disgusting.

I tried on an old pair of jeans

and couldn't get them past my knees!

I was like, Great, this is all I need.

Defective knees.

you can be sure someone will

always be praying for you.

And it's someone who likes you

a whole lot, so that oughta

count for a little extra!

I have not stopped giving thanks for
you, remembering you in my prayers.

EPHESIANS 1:16 NIV

I like to put on some soothing music,

take a long hot bath, call up a

good friend like you...

and do some major whining.

Thanks for listening.

If women ran Hollywood...
meaningful dialogue and poignant
love scenes would be featured
in slow-motion instant replays.

Friends don't let friends

walk around all day with

something stuck in their teeth.

Pagers, cell phones, answering machines...

It's getting easier to hear God's

"still, small voice" these days—

It's the only one not preceded

by a "Beep!"

Your friendship...

It's the most uplifting thing

in my life without underwire.

I like having you to talk to.

You just listen with an open mind.

You don't try
to "fix things."
No offense, but
you'd make a
lousy man.

I feel so close to you I would

give you the shirt off my back,

the roof over my head,

the shoes from my feet...

Just don't get any ideas about

my coupon collection.

On those days when I feel like screaming—

I usually do. Try to stay out of earshot.

I'm learning not to sweat the small stuff.

But not being friends with you,

now that I would have to sweat.

Promise me that when we're

old ladies, we'll still get together

to talk and laugh the way we do now.

And promise you'll tell me if spit gathers

at the corners of my mouth.

I hate that!

A GIRLFRIEND...

won't just "be there" for you in a crisis.

She'll hang around while you wait

for an appliance to be delivered.

If you or I had been Lot's wife,

we'd never have risked looking back

and turning into a pillar of salt.

Imagine how you'd retain water!

We've had joy, we've had fun...

We've had cheesecake by the ton...

Thanks for some great memories!